Strength in numbers

A deeper understanding of yourself and others with the Enneagram

Enneagram Insights Publishing

Amanda Maney & Rachel Watson

Published in 2019 by

Enneagram Insights
Publishing

www.powerofpersonality.com

ISBN: 978-0-9930852-3-9

For everyone who is curious to deepen their understanding of the Enneagram.

Contents

Foreword

Foreword

Back in 2015, Amanda Maney and Rachel Watson reached out to me, asking me to write the foreword for their first book, Personality Portraits: The Enneagram Encountered. The truth is, I hesitated at first. Although I'd been deeply involved in the personal development, spiritual and self-help industry for almost fifteen years, and had the privilege to work on some of the most groundbreaking books of our time, I'd never really connected with the Enneagram. On several occasions, enthusiasts of the approach had taken me to one side, attempting to explain it to me—passionately sharing what they knew—but it didn't really click with me at that time. That perspective changed when Personality Portraits landed on my desk.

The first book was a simply explained—yet deeply profound—introduction to the Enneagram. What struck me instantly was not only the depth of knowledge portrayed in the book, but the ability to convey it effectively through diagrams and illustrations. The different communication styles and characteristic behaviors were carefully explained, and then made immediately apparent through the illustrations. In the time that it took me to read the book, I was transported into the world of the Enneagram, and I not only conceptually understood it, but felt the experience of it for the first time. As someone who has the privilege of reading, reviewing, and creating a vast number of books, I instantly recognized Personality Portraits as the kind of book I have the most respect for: one that is created with the audience in mind, and shares knowledge and wisdom in a way that is easily received by the reader.

By the time this second book—Strength in Numbers—landed on my desk, I couldn't wait to see how Maney and Watson had evolved this work. I was curious to see how they would build on the last book, and whether they would be able to keep to their original simplicity while deepening the readers knowledge further. Within a few minutes of reading, I realized they had not only succeeded in this aim, but greatly surpassed it.

Strength in Numbers delivers exactly what it promises in its subtitle: A deeper understanding of yourself and others through the Enneagram. Whether you want to: fundamentally understand your response to stress so you can navigate it more effectively; learn more about your "triad connections," and how you can find strength and stability in them; discover the "Wing Effect" and how you are affected by your neighbouring types; grasp your direction of movement; or discover your "primal drives" and your instinctive core comfort zones, this book has you covered. It not only takes all these individual components, but looks at how they work in tandem. This gifts you with a system that is not just interesting as a theory, but that can be applied in your everyday life to enable you to operate optimally.

Although I'm obviously not an expert in the Enneagram, my expertise does lie in being able to spot a great book. Once again, Maney and Watson have created a book that has the potential to be a classic for years to come. It's readability and accessibility mean that it's a great starting point for a beginner. I imagine it would also be an invaluable resource for experienced practitioners and their clients too.

So, whether you are just starting out with your Enneagram journey, or are a seasoned practitioner with a host of clients, this unique book with its carefully illustrated content will be one that you refer to time and time again.

Sasha Allenby - Ghostwriter, Publishing Consultant, and Author of Write an Evolutionary Self-Help Book: The Definitive Guide for Spiritual Entrepreneurs

Prefaces

Prefaces

What a delight it is to take readers deeper into this beautiful work. And how grateful I am to be doing this with such a powerful advocate and role model of life lived to the full! Rachel continues to inspire me, as she has since our first connection; our work together is a source of unceasing joy as people's lives transform with the insights and revelations it brings. Heartfelt thanks to all who have shared such powerful reflections with us - your experiences touch the lives of all who encounter them.

We know the value this material brings; we see the transformation of individuals, organisations and communities as the work unfolds - I am excited for you and with you as you journey onwards - enjoy!

Amanda

On receiving such positive feedback about Book 1, coupled with our desire to provide greater depth on this powerful personality descriptor, Amanda and I embarked on researching our own particular findings about each of the personality types. I have thoroughly enjoyed the journey of writing the second book, with Amanda. Thank you so much Amanda!

I continue to be fascinated by human behaviour, our patterns, our subtle differences and this tool has become an intrinsic part of the work I deliver in both the corporate world and with my personal clients.

Thank you to all who have shared their stories and experiences, you know who you are and I am so grateful for your honesty in sharing your map of the world.

I hope you enjoy reading this book, as much as I enjoyed writing it!

Rachel

Our promise to you:

This book will deepen your understanding of yourself and your behaviours, providing you with a balance between 'an interesting and insightful read' and practical ideas to enhance your own particular strengths.

Introduction

Welcome back!

The fact that you are here, reading book two, means you are 'in', so we need say very little to get launched into 'Strength in Numbers'. Do you now find yourself unable to watch any TV programme without typing every character? Have conversations with friends turned into heated debates over drivers and behaviours and which type your respective mothers / fathers / partners / children etc.... might be? Perhaps you have had some "Aha!" moments where you realise why that particular colleague is such a challenge, why that family member causes so much upset? Wherever you may be up to, you will inevitably have questions, lots of them, and you are ready to enjoy taking your understanding to the next level.

In this book we will be feasting on the nuances and subtleties that make the Enneagram so rich and diverse. We will explore the aspects and connections which make sense of the apparent overlaps and similarities you see. The combination of perspectives, the ways in which different situations bring certain responses from particular types – this adds depth and movement to the impressionist painting to which we introduced you in book 1.

The impressionist painting is a helpful metaphor here – the whole needs to be seen at a distance to be fully understood and appreciated. Understanding the Enneagram is a cumulative, organic process. It is important not to 'hang your hat' on any single piece of information but to let it blend, meld and distil into deep meaning and truth.

Features and Frailties

- A quiz, to take you deeper

Features and Frailties - A quiz, to take you deeper

Our starting point is going to add some layers to your understanding of the types by exploring and comparing their communication styles, characteristic behaviours, likely avoidances and pitfalls. We invite you to challenge your own understanding by completing the table at the start of each section and then comparing your answers with the explanation that follows. In each case, there is one 'best fit' option for each type. You may find that you fill in the numbers you find easiest and leave the 'unsures' out. This is helpful in itself as it clarifies your current level of understanding and then directs you to go a little deeper.

In giving you the answers and explanations we have grouped the types into their centres. It is important to remember that the key driver for each centre is fundamental. For heart types, everything stems from their need for love and attention. Head types seek safety, gut types want control. It is important to remember that the drivers of all personality traits and behaviours are subconscious - and may not be known at a conscious level.

Communication style:

You can often spot types, especially if they are out of balance, just by the way they speak: see what styles you recognise in those around you...

COMMUNICATION STYLE					
Preaching		**Lecturing**		**Risk assessing**	
Lamenting		**Boasting**		**Flattery, advice giving**	
Storytelling		**Dominating**		**Circumlocuting, wordy repeating**	

2 – The Helper:
Flattery / advice giving – 2s want others to feel good about themselves and to see the 2 as a catalyst for that. This feeds their need to be needed.

3 – The Achiever:
Boasting – 3s are the consummate self publicists, for them this generates acknowledgement and respect.

4 – The Individualist:
Lamenting – 4s are drawn to the pain in any situation, the creative expression of which gives them their unique perspective.

5 – The Forensic:
Lecturing – 5s seek to acquire information in order to feel safe. They connect through in depth, lengthy expositions of the knowledge they have accumulated.

6 – The Teammate:
Risk-assessing – 6s will invariably be seeking security by weighing up the possible risks and dangers of any ventures, investing in constant 'pro-ing' and 'con-ing' of life.

7 – The Adventurer:
Storytelling – Embellishment is the forte of the 7, ever making the most of any opportunity to entertain in order to avoid the anathema of a boring moment.

8 – The Champion:
Dominating – 8s are powerful communicators – their tone of voice alone conveys strength and determination, giving them potential control of any conversation.

9 – The Peacemaker:
Circumlocuting, wordy repetition - 9s are as ready to listen as to speak, their gentle tones and diplomacy soothe and persuade, preserving a sense of harmony.

1 – The Reformer:
Preaching - 1s speak with strength and conviction; their desire to drive reform creates urgency and commands respect - clipped tones and a passionate restraint conveys their call to improve.

Characteristic behaviour:

These behaviours will certainly show up when types are under pressure, each one trying to cope with stress and meet their needs.

CHARACTERISTIC BEHAVIOUR					
Taking charge		**Self-promotion**		**Seeking harmony**	
Seeking perfection, integrity		**Being unique**		**Observing, acquiring knowledge**	
Helping others		**Constant activity**		**Questioning, seeking security**	

2 – The Helper
Helping others - The desire to be indispensable drives 2s to help and to serve - and feel loved in return.

3 – The Achiever
Self-promotion - The quest for respect drives image-focused behaviours; 3s seek to show themselves at their best - and make sure others have noticed!

4 – The Individualist
Being unique - Seeking to be 'different' fuels a passionate flame of contrast - fully lit or almost extinguished, with nothing much in between.

5 – The Forensic
Observing, acquiring knowledge - Focused and dispassionate, 5s are logical fact-seekers, in passionate pursuit of ALL the information in their fields of interest.

6 – The Teammate
Questioning, seeking security - Always checking for danger, heightened instinctual vigilance drives a desire for safe structures and internal or external orderliness.

7 – The Adventurer
Constant activity - An insatiable desire for busy-ness has them constantly on the go; seeking future excitement can lead to chaos in 'the now'.

8 – The Champion
Taking charge - A major force in their world, bulldozing all resistance, 8s move mountains with passion and power; their energy makes them invincible.

9 – The Peacemaker
Seeking harmony – Easy-going and tolerant, 9s will 'go with the flow', seeing all perspectives and sacrificing self to keep the peace.

1 – The Reformer:
Seeking perfection, integrity – scrupulously honest and fiercely principled; 1s are driven by an unrelenting moral code: they must do the right thing and do it right.

Avoidance:

Remember that each personality type is built around the need to avoid one pivotal experience, which the subconscious fears as much as death.

AVOIDANCE					
Exposure		**Being ordinary**		**Imperfection**	
Own needs		**Chaos & change**		**Failure**	
Confrontation		**Pain**		**Weakness**	

2 – The Helper
Own needs – 2s are driven to meet the needs of others: they refuse to acknowledge that they have any needs of their own.

3 – The Achiever
Failure – 3s' desire for glory leads them to hide their failures along the way; they will deceive if necessary to avoid being seen as anything less than the best.

4 – The Individualist
Being ordinary - Needing to be different, over-emphasising the emotion of their own experience rescues 4s from the mundane: being ordinary attracts no attention.

5 – The Forensic
Exposure - Safe in their 'information fortress', 5s will do all they can to avoid emotional exposure, which would reveal their full vulnerability to the world.

6 – The Teammate
Chaos and change - Needing structure or predictability to feel secure, 6s organise themselves and others to eliminate chaos and change, lest the rules of life be broken.

7 – The Adventurer
Pain - To feel safe, 7s need the promise of something exciting to come, in order to avoid the possibility of feeling pain in 'the now'.

8 – The Champion
Weakness - For 8s attack is the best form of defence: taking charge is the only option - showing weakness threatens their ability to control.

9 – The Peacemaker
Confrontation - Control of self is paramount to a 9, who will go to extremes to preserve composure, rather than risk confrontation which could lead to disconnection and loss of control.

1 – The Reformer
Imperfection - Controlling life in the pursuit of external principles, imperfection could lead to being judged and found wanting - an anathema to a 1.

Pitfalls:

When each type is at its worst, you will see the most negative behaviours arise as they revert to their own particular pitfall.

PITFALLS					
Sloth		**Pride**		**Greed**	
Deceit		**Lust**		**Judgement**	
Fear/Worry		**Gluttony**		**Envy**	

2 – The Helper
Pride – Conscious of everyone else's needs, ignoring their own, 2s have a subconscious sense of superiority – they take an almost haughty pride in denying themselves and serving others.

3 – The Achiever
Deceit – Creating an impressive image, the need to succeed drives 3s to deceive - at least by over-embellishment and bragging – they will lie to to secure the prize.

4 – The Individualist
Envy – Complaining woefully about the unfairness of their lot, 4s feel they have been dealt a bad hand by fate: they envy others their good fortune and bemoan their lack of it.

5 – The Forensic
Greed – Packrat, bunker mentality drives 5s to hoard – they become stingy and mean, locking down their own stores for fear of being left without.

6 – The Teammate
Fear/Worry – Panic drives 6s towards paranoia and irrational thinking – a conspiracy mentality can sweep them into interpreting every happening as a threat, every stimulus as an omen of impending misfortune.

7 – The Adventurer
Gluttony – Stuffing themselves manically with all the goodies they can extract from life – their craving for stimulation creates an exhausting, over-indulgent, never-ending quest for excitement.

8 – The Champion
Lust – Consuming the whole of life, possessing things, people and places to make them their own, 8s suck everything in with the sheer force of their determination to control.

9 – The Peacemaker
Sloth – Refusal to engage with life leads 9s into an internal inertia – they deteriorate into lazy lumps of stuck energy.

1 – The Reformer
Judgement – Harsh and sharp, 1s find fault with everyone and everything; they criticise and condemn in their certainty that they are right and that others should measure up accordingly.

Under Pressure

Under Pressure

How do you manage needs and stresses?

The social styles of each personality emerge from the way they get their needs met, how they respond to stress and their 'primal drives' (see chapter of same name).

We can describe, in general terms, how the types tend to respond to perceived needs and stresses.

These descriptors are broad brush strokes, describing general behaviour patterns rather than specific instances. They are useful as sieves to separate out personalities that might seem similar but have key differences in these areas.

You may find yourself more drawn to some personalities than others; this can be a result of the way your personality approaches its needs and stressors.

MEETING NEEDS

Demand	Earn	Withdraw
3	1	4
7	2	5
8	6	9

REACTING TO STRESS

Optimistic	Expressive	Objective
2	4	1
7	6	3
9	8	5

Getting needs met

There are three approaches to getting needs met: the types will tend to predominantly favour one. Three types will tend to **demand** to get their needs met. Three types will try to **earn** their way and three types will tend to **withdraw** to get what they need.

Demand: 3s, 7s and 8s

Demanders generate high impact which reinforces their presence and 'pushes against' whatever exists. This is about making whoever is there aware of their (ego) need - they want their audience to know that they are there and to know what they want.

Earn: 1s, 2s and 6s

Earners move 'towards' in an attitude of service in order to have their own needs met. This service can be personal, affiliation or cause based; it does not attempt to make impact on the audience but rather to comply with either internal or external principles or rules.

Withdraw: 4s, 5s and 9s

These types tend to move 'away' in order to meet their own needs. They may do this externally - by physically retreating and/or internally by withdrawing to their inner space thereby detaching themselves from their surroundings. They create daydreams and fantasies about their reality, or retreat completely from it.

To add some depth to these descriptions, we will take our personalities to a rest break in a workplace or training event and see how they might respond to their desire for coffee...

Demanders

3s will make themselves busy and important – they will attract the admiration of others and will probably ask someone to get their coffee for them. Even though coffee is available in situ, they are more likely to inspire someone to go the extra mile: "I don't do queues; be a dear and just pick me up a latte would you? Skinny, decaff, with gingerbread syrup and a chocolate stirrer.... Don't go to that scruffy café on the corner – you don't mind going to the new designer diner do you?"

7s will turn their desire for coffee into an opportunity to entertain – and the coffee becomes the applause. They may turn a cartwheel, tell a joke or relate the latest hilarious tale: the whole break becomes a show and the audience fall over themselves to bring the coffee to them.

8s will have made their coffee needs loudly known from the start of the day and others will run to meet them. Their coffee will be ready before anyone else's and will be delivered to their hand... or else!

Earners

2s see how needy the group is and spend the coffee break getting coffee for others. They are likely to wind up without any coffee themselves; they may even find themselves helping to clear up after the break, but in such a way as to have their sacrifice appreciated.

6s will work unobtrusively to get their group's coffee needs met. Within the group, they ensure that the rules of hierarchy are respected; those with positions of authority or social respect get their coffee first and due deference is shown to all positions.

Where they will be judged for the course outcomes, 1s will only accept the coffee break if they feel they have worked sufficiently hard to deserve it; they will show tight-lipped disapproval if they have not earned their rest.

Withdrawers

4s will take themselves away from the group, possibly feeling somewhat unsettled or ill at ease, they will not be where others are... but they will hope that someone will notice – and bring coffee with concern for their (particular and very special) needs.

5s will tend to absent themselves completely during the break – preferably reading ahead with their own flask of coffee (you never know when supplies will run out).

For 9s, coffee will appear with least energy expended – either via a well-trained friend, or by nipping in first or last to acquire coffee without queueing! They will have found the perfect place to enjoy the break – perhaps the comfortable couch for a chance to connect up with others or to recharge with a beautiful window view.

Responding to stress

There are three general responses to difficult situations, which come from **optimistic**, **expressive** and **objective** stances subconsciously adopted by the types when under stress. As with meeting needs, the types will tend to favour one response.

Optimistic

2s, 7s and 9s are more likely to approach life's challenges optimistically, with a sense of everything working out well, reframing disappointment or difficulty and looking for the silver lining to every cloud.

Expressive

4s, 6s and 8s will 'say it like it is', reacting emotionally to conflict and challenge and wanting others to respond by matching their emotional state.

Objective

1s, 3s and 5s strive to put personal feelings to one side in order to solve problems dispassionately, prioritising efficiency and competence under pressure.

To illustrate these stances, we can picture the types' responses to the crisis of the sinking Titanic...

Optimists

2s' optimism springs from the fact that they 'know' they are set up to meet any need. They will be funnelling people to lifeboats and giving out blankets and life jackets – "I can save you and you need me with you on the life boat... you wouldn't cope without me at sea..."

7s' need to avoid pain drives them to keep things light, even when disaster strikes. They would entertain as the ship went down to take everyone's mind off the crisis – "As long as we can laugh and joke, we will all be fine... somehow..."

9s might sleep through much of the event ... emerging from the cabin scratching their heads. "What crisis?" Their response, once realisation dawns, will be to try to avoid letting the crisis affect them, buffering the emotions and chaos as best they can.

Expressives

4s, predisposed to feel the extremes of human emotion, will become melodramatic in the extreme – somehow their experience is far worse than anyone else's – they will feel and describe the intensity of the pain more fully than the less sensitive – lamenting all the while - "How could this happen to ME?"

6s, constantly on the alert for danger, are compelled to sound the alarm for the group. Overtly ill at ease, they may sound complaining. They would insist: the etiquette for abandoning ship MUST be followed. (In reality, they probably would not have embarked on the ship in the first place – too few lifeboats - they would have alerted the appropriate authorities.)

8s feel a huge sense of responsibility for 'their people' and need to take charge, showing strength and controlling every situation. They would rage overtly at the fools whose fault this was, making short work of anyone in their way – commanding others to "Just DO it!"

Objectives

3s' belief that they can succeed in any situation will create a strategic approach. They will want to step away from any emotions which might obstruct the goal. Cool in a crisis, they will use all means necessary to make it onto a lifeboat. With every move objectively calculated, they will pick the best passengers and crew to accompany them to optimise their chances of success.

5s' belief that knowledge will keep them safe will have driven them to research survival at sea. Avoiding emotional distraction, their strategy would be to use logic to think their way out of danger. Calm and self-sufficient, they would create their own survival kit, to take them to safety with absolutely no need for anybody else's help.

1s' need to do the right thing generates a need to control themselves in a crisis. A strong, external set of principles will direct their actions: they may feel responsible for the lives of all the vulnerable on board - the old, the young and the infirm. They will try to maintain objectivity in order to control the crowd, expecting others to behave 'as they should', in accordance with those principles, which they expect others to share.

The Triads

The Triads
Find strength and stability in your triad connections

We now need to look into variation subtleties which arise from the connections between types and the influences of the types on each other. We liken this to looking closer at an impressionist painting: the fine "brush strokes" will reveal apparent contradictions - the closer we look, the more variation we will see.

What do we mean by 'directions of movement'?

The collective wisdom of the Enneagram over many, many years indicates that each type has a particularly strong connection with two other types. Whilst, of course, we can all demonstrate the full range of human behaviours, we will tend to 'do' more of certain types' behaviours than others; this is not random.

We talk about one type 'moving towards' these other two types and in doing so, adopting more of their kind of behaviours, becoming more like them, superficially at least. There are slight differences in the suggestions around how healthy these 'directions of movement' are for each type. We have our own experience and teaching on this subject, which matches some teachers and differs from others.

In terms of the directions of movement between types, there is a greater distinction, between our work and the work generally found in other books or training programmes offered on the Enneagram. So, what makes us take a different view?

Our experience with people has led us to a different understanding of the connections. This understanding has been tried and tested over many years and has been shown to have significant impact as it offers the balance needed to bring the best out of each type.

We describe the connected types as three triads. Each type in one centre has strong connection with a specific type in both of the other two centres. Heart, head and gut are linked. This brings balance to every type.

Explore the triads and you will see the richness they bring. Looking at each type within the triad for their main gifts and challenges shows how well balanced they become as they access the strengths of the other two triad types.

The diagram shows the gifts of each type outside the circle and their two main challenges inside it. The lines indicate the possibility of going in either direction. The movement between types can be constructive or destructive: types can access the strengths of their triad connections but they can also adopt their frailties.

The Enneagram Triads

9 – 6 – 3 The Chameleons

These three types have a reason to be particularly good at adopting the behaviours of the personalities around them and looking like other types. This behaviour is adaptive, chameleon-like, these types are more likely than most to change with their social surroundings. The reasons are different for each type – 9s seek harmony, morphing to maintain rapport, 6s blend in to be part of the team, conforming to agreed etiquette, 3s impress, adopting the group's behaviours to ensure success.

These three personality types have strong connection with each other and, more than the other two triads, these three will tend to operate out of each other's centres a great deal, looking very much like each other. They are a little like the earth element, the versatile soil, planet's skin, constantly working and moving to accommodate changing pressures - the foundation of life.

Healthy Directions 9 – 6 – 3

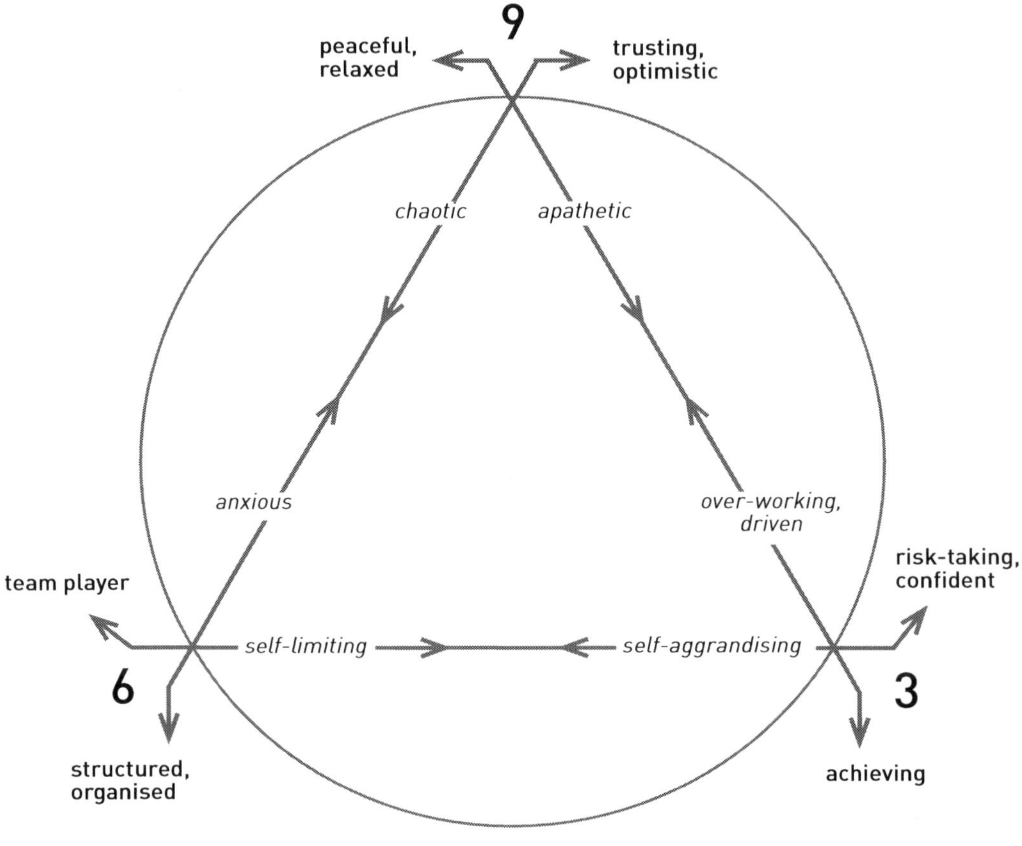

Destructive connections:

9s can find themselves adopting the anxious and self limiting behaviours of the unhealthy 6 when out of balance. They can become paranoid, risk averse and rigid, fearing chaos and looking for someone to take charge and restore harmony. Equally, the 9 can become work driven and/or self-aggrandising, like the unhealthy 3 - 'bigging up' their contribution to the task at hand in order to stay 'in' with the crowd.

6s can slump into chaotic, apathetic, 9-like behaviour when overwhelmed. adopting a helpless, victim stance and deferring all responsibility to others. They can also move to 3, becoming task driven, following the letter of the law to the limits and can be drawn into aggressively competitive self-aggrandising.

3s can exhibit the anxiety and self limiting behaviour of the 6 when threatened by failure - their aversion to humiliation can lead them to drop projects or people suddenly and go into hiding. They can also fall into 9-like chaos and apathy when schemes are foiled and they are deprived of the success and adulation they crave.

Constructive connections:

A 9 will find two main challenges: becoming chaotic – in which case moving to the **structured, methodical, organisational skills** of the 6, is hugely beneficial – or becoming apathetic – in which case the **achieving, goal and success orientation** of the 3 is a great antidote, injecting energy and enthusiasm.

6s will struggle with anxiety: feeling that life is full of potential threat – in which case the **trusting optimism** of the 9 is a perfect balm – or becoming self-limiting through fear – in which case the **risk-taking confidence** of the 3 is the counterbalance they need.

3s are likely to overwork, becoming driven to achieve – the **peaceful, relaxed stance** of the 9 balances this beautifully – or they will self-aggrandise in order to impress others – the **team player** stance of the 6 counteracts this by grounding them in the need to remember there are no 'self-made-men'.

7 – 4 – 1 The Visionaries

Each of these three types has a forward focused, creative energy - they hold the vision of how the world could be. Again, this comes from different drivers - 7s expand possibilities, creating exciting futures to avoid boredom; 4s' creative vision comes from their unique view of the world; 1s need to reform the world, seeing instantly how everything could be improved.

These types share an energy - akin to the wind, restless, changeable, making all things new and reshaping the landscape as it goes. Looking, as with the Chameleons, at each type within the triad for their main gifts and challenges shows how well balanced they become as they access the strengths of the other two types.

Healthy Directions 7 – 4 – 1

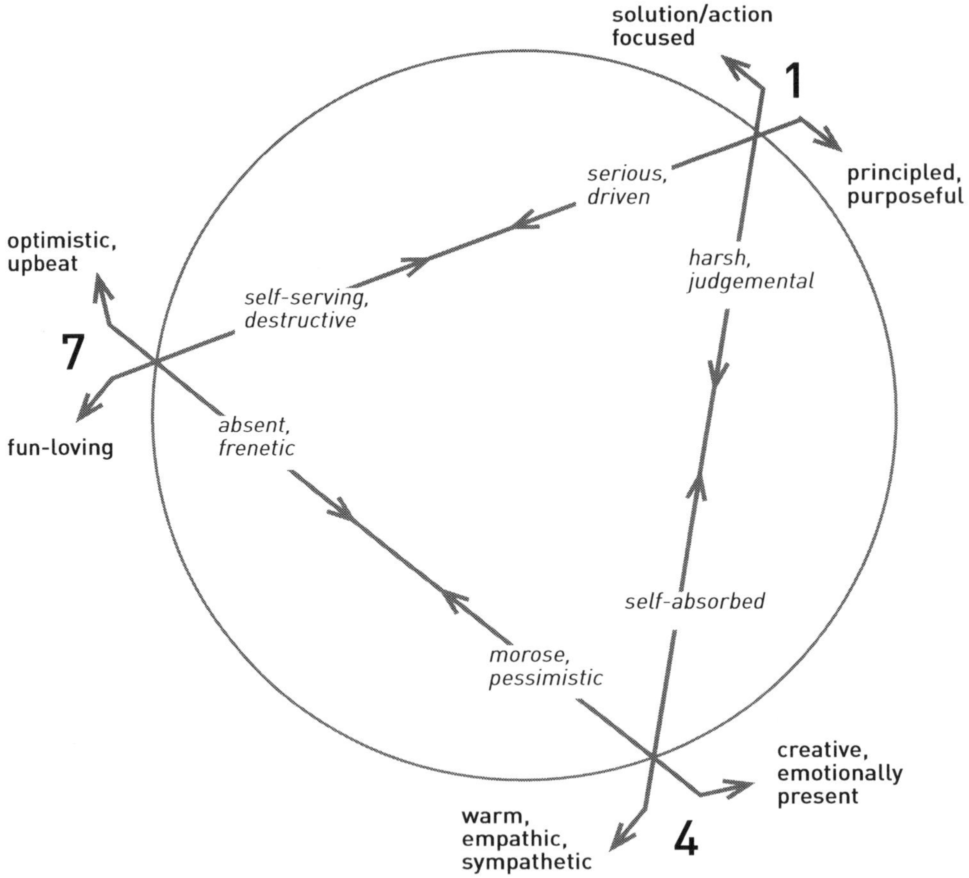

Destructive connections:

7s can lose their playfulness in seeking stimulation, taking on the serious, 'driven-ness' of the 1; they can then become self-righteous, judging others and themselves harshly. Extreme drives for stimulation in 7s can be followed by morose, pessimistic, self-absorbed phases of energy depletion and bleak mood: when drained, they adopt the unhealthy behaviours of the 4.

1s can move to the self-serving, destructive behaviours of the 7; generally still under the banner of the righteous cause, but resulting in absent freneticism, lost in 'busy-ness', seeking approval by 'doing' constantly, without rest. They can also fall into 4-like low moods, the self-absorbed, morose pessimism showing through in a 'woe is me' lament for the sacrifices they make to do the right thing.

4s can become very cause driven, serious, harsh and judgemental, like the unhealthy 1. They see themselves not only as different and special but also superior, as others fail to live up to their standards and expectations. 4s will also tend towards the absent, frenetic behaviour of the 7, seeking consolation for their acutely felt pain in self-serving, destructive behaviours.

Constructive connections:

Challenges for the 7: they can become self serving and destructive in their search for novelty and pleasure - in which case the **principled purpose** of the 1 is a grounding influence. If they are becoming absent and frenetic, the **creative, emotionally present** stance of the 4 is the perfect foil.

1s struggle with seriousness, becoming driven to serve their cause - **the fun-loving, playful** nature of the 7 is just what they need, to bring levity and joy back into focus. If the 1 is becoming harsh and judgemental in their compulsion to 'do it right', the **warmth** of the 4 brings **empathy** and **sympathy** - for self and others.

4s can become self-absorbed in their sense of being different and feeling the pain of the world - they focus on their own woes exclusively. This is the time for their connection to the 1 stance to bring them to outward-facing, **solution-focused** thinking and taking action to aid others, a 'cause' other than their own. If a 4 is becoming morose and pessimistic, the **upbeat optimism** of the forward-thinking 7 redresses the balance wonderfully.

8 – 5 – 2 The Challengers

The energy of this triad is high impact, rather like fire in the earth, wind and fire trilogy. Commanding attention, it is full of raw power to create change. These three types have a strength about them; they challenge the status quo. They are ready to take on the world to achieve what is needed.

This comes from different motivations: 8s thrive on glorious combat, pitting their strength against the odds; 5s, the Forensics, delight in taking the world apart to find out more; 2s will take on any adversary to provide for their own. Once again, we see the balance playing out across the triad as each type gives and takes benefit from the others, each offering the perfect antidote to the possible fragilities of the others.

Healthy Directions 8 – 5 – 2

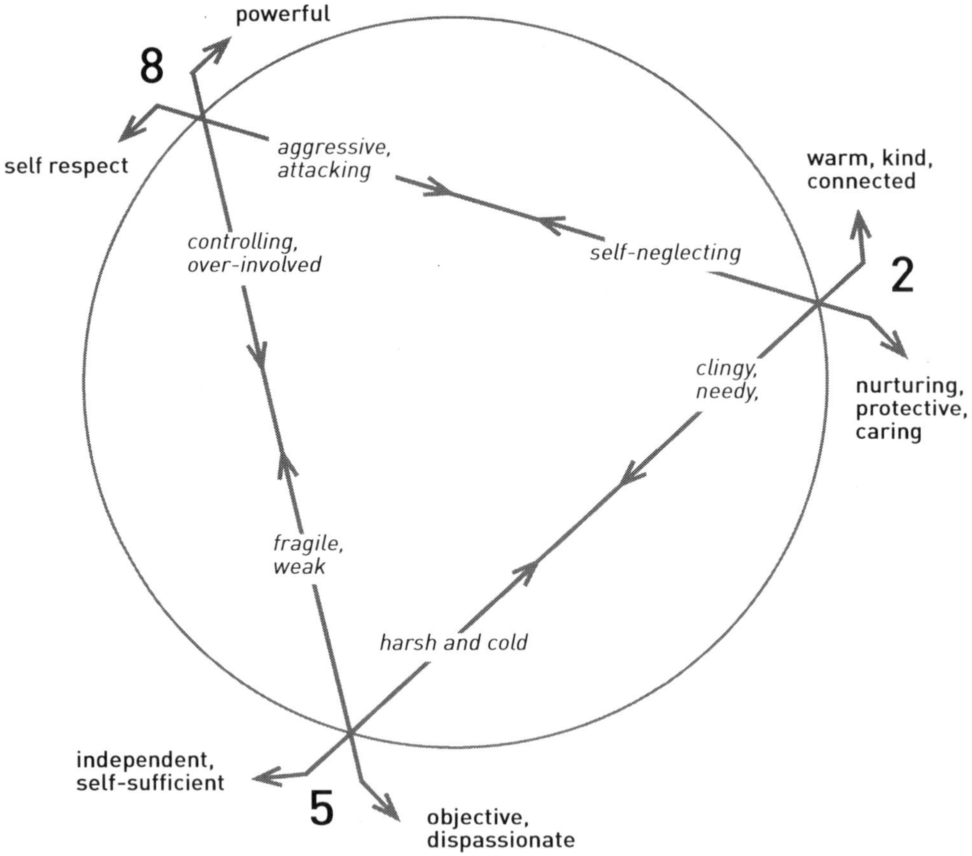

Destructive connections:

8s can become unexpectedly 2-like, clingy and needy, neglecting their basic needs and smothering their people as they battle against others. They may feel fragile and weak - like 5s - which drives them to present as all powerful. They can adopt the harsh coldness of the 5 as they objectively study the weaknesses of the opposition to plan their defeat.

2s, when out of balance, may become 8-like - aggressive and attacking, controlling and over-involving themselves in the lives of those they feel to be showing too little appreciation or need. They may adopt a more 5-like stance when redundancy threatens - fragile and weak, they may become harsh and cold, calculating ways to force others to depend on them.

5s can become 8-like in aggressive, attacking exchanges, using their huge knowledge store to defeat or belittle others, when they feel themselves to be under threat. 5s can look 2-like, neglecting their own needs, if unhealthy in their quest to know it all. They can become clingy and needy - seeking protection from others when feeling unsafe.

Constructive connections:

The 8's tendency towards aggressive attack is tempered beautifully by the **nurturing** of the **protective and caring** 2. Controlling, over-involved behaviour is relinquished when the 8 adopts the **objectivity** and **dispassionate** stance of the 5.

2s can neglect self in their drive to meet others' needs, in which case the healthy **self-respect** of the 8 is the ideal counterbalance. When 2s are inclined towards clingy neediness, the **independence** and **self-sufficiency** of the 5 serves them well.

5s can feel fragile and weak in the world - they find power in their ability to adopt the **strength** of the 8. When they become cold and harsh in their drive for data over dreams, the 5 finds **warmth** and **kindness** in the connection of the 2 with the emotional needs of self and others.

These directions of movement can be consciously used. Bringing ourselves back to our best self is much easier when we know the 'symptoms' most likely to indicate a problem and can choose the appropriate 'antidote' by simply adopting the stance of the type most likely to restore balance.

Equally, where we know each other's triads and patterns, we can call others into more resourceful modes of behaviour just by inviting them to change perspective. This can become an easy short-cut to a more resourceful state. We can offer a speedy, light-hearted response - a rescue remedy, if you will - in a moment of need. We can also consciously build resilience, increasing sustainability by strategically drawing on the strengths of the triad.

The 'Wing' Effect

The 'Wing' Effect
- How much are you influenced by your neighbour types?

Which wing are you?

The layering of personality continues with the 'wing' effect. In addition to the directions of movement linking us to other types in other triads, our behaviour is further influenced by the personality type on either side of us on the Enneagram circle. Our experience tells us that some individuals have more of a leaning to one wing than another, others are influenced by both wings equally, others again will say they are influenced by one wing only, or not at all. Is it any wonder, that there are so many rich facets to our dynamic, unique personalities?

When describing the wing influences, then, we will refer to the most extreme, the simplest version of the wing effects. The reality is that this is more of a continuum. You may well find yourself identifying with some aspects of both of the wings described here; you may find that your behaviours change, depending on environment.

We have also noticed that one wing tends to bring more reserve, whilst the other brings more emotional openness – each wing continuum moves from a quieter, more serious end to a noisier, more playful end.

This variation reminds us of the Enneagram message - we need the balance that the diversity brings.

Remember that these wing descriptions are the broad brushstrokes of the painting - allow yourself to connect with what works for you and to let go of anything that doesn't. Some will find clearer definition in what follows; others may not resonate with the wing effects at all.

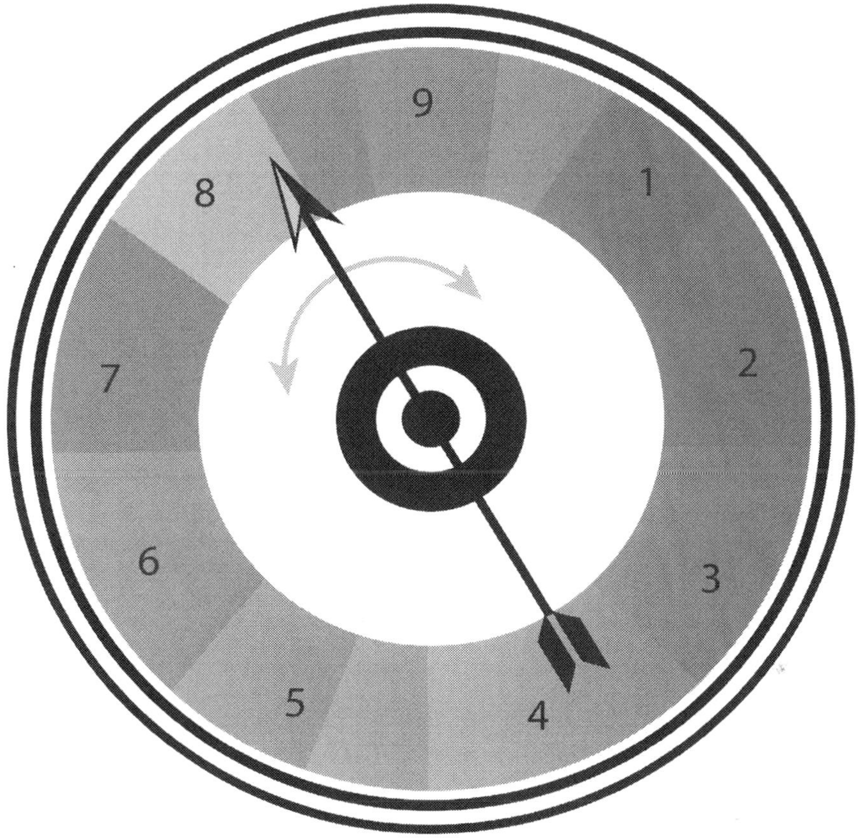
9
1
2
3
4
5
6
7
8

The Helper

2:1s

Core type: 2 - has a fundamental need to be needed, in order to be loved.

Influenced by: 1 - has an additional drive to do the right thing, to control - to be good enough.

Doing the right thing in order to be needed draws 2:1s towards public service and the caring professions, where they can show love and be loved through serving others.

Acknowledgement, for a 2:1, can be quieter and more understated; they are more emotionally restrained. They do not need effusive thanks, a simple note will mean the world to them. Something inside them wants to know that they have made a difference and it could not have been done without them.

The 1 need to be good enough will influence 2:1s into greater seriousness and sense of purpose in their quest for love. Principles and morality will be important to them as they strive to save the world.

2:3s

Core type: 2 - has a fundamental need to be needed, in order to be loved.

Influenced by: 3 - has an additional drive to achieve and be successful, in order to be respected.

Being respected in order to be needed draws 2:3s towards helping in roles with higher profile or status, personal or professional, where they can show love and be loved through helping others to achieve.

Acknowledgement, for a 2:3, needs to be louder and more demonstrative; they are more openly emotional. They thrive on public displays of gratitude and affection; they will give everything for the badge of honour you bestow upon them. In their heart of hearts, they know you can't live without them.

The 3 need for success will influence 2:3s into more playfulness and desire for applause in their quest for love. Appreciation and accomplishment will be important to them as they provide for every need.

The Achiever

3:2s

Core type: 3 - has a fundamental need to achieve and be successful, in order to be respected.

Influenced by: 2 - has an additional drive to be needed, in order to be loved.

Wanting to be needed in order to achieve draws 3:2s towards audience adulation, private or public; they seek to dazzle and impress, by fulfilling desires. In this way, they attract respect through meeting others' needs.

Acknowledgement, for a 3:2, requires applause and accolade; they live for the fanfare and razzamatazz. Openly revelling in the "Wow!" factor, 3:2s thrive on competition; they will give their all for fame and glory, they love to satisfy the crowd. Winning thrills them; they want others to see them as the best of the best.

The 2 need for appreciation will influence 3:2s into more connection with the opinion of others - they will engage more with their audience in their desire for respect. Making others feel good will be important to them; their generosity knows no bounds, as they set themselves up for ultimate success.

3:4s

Core type: 3 - has a fundamental need to achieve and be successful, in order to be respected.

Influenced by: 4 - has an additional drive to be special or different, in order to be noticed.

The desire to be special or different in order to achieve, tends to take 3:4s towards success in their endeavours - in the home or workplace, in the professional fields, where achievement is all about impressing select audiences with a unique product or performance.

Acknowledgement then comes through awards and trophies; the specialness of 3:4s seeks recognition, and yet requires a slightly more exclusive context – not so much a glitzy parade as an elegant, star-filled presentation evening. To be admired for their style and class satisfies the 4-like need to be seen as unique as well as the core 3 desire to succeed.

The 4 influence on the 3 will make them slightly more reserved, more serious and they will direct their efforts towards pleasing a sophisticated audience.

Being somewhat maverick, or off the beaten track will appeal, just as long as there is clear success to be had.

The Individualist

4:3s

Core type: 4 - has a fundamental drive to be special or different, in order to be noticed.

Influenced by: 3 - has an additional need to achieve and be successful, in order to be respected.

The desire to be successful, connects the 4 with an audience. Whilst they need to be special, they also want their unique creativity to be admired. They are stylishly sophisticated; there is something superior, almost aristocratic about this type of 4.

Acknowledgement for a 4:3 will ideally be a refined affair, with modest but classy tokens of admiration. Not showy but definitely more of an exclusive event; they delight in lavish extravagance but let there be nothing ordinary about it.

The 3 influence on the 4 brings a lightness and sense of fun; 4:3s are more likely to be found partying with the 'hoi polloi', although distinctive dress or star status will invariably pick them out from the crowd.

4:5s

Core type: 4 - has a fundamental drive to be special or different, in order to be noticed.

Influenced by: 5 - has an additional need to be knowledgeable, in order to be safe.

The need for knowledge makes the 4:5 more issue based in the drive to be unique. There is a deep empathy; their quest for information is focused by awareness of the flawed nature of life. Their 5 influence brings a sharp intuition.

Acknowledgement for 4:5s is a private, sensitive moment in time - they are more uncomfortable with conventional events. Bohemian in style, theirs is the spirit of the tortured artist; the rebel without a cause resides here. Emotional authenticity is everything to the 4:5; originality will not be sacrificed for the benefit of others.

The 5 influence on the 4 brings out in them the exquisite poignancy of life; a sense of the tragic and a connection with select groups of like-minded people with the courage to embrace the full extremes of life experience.

The Forensic

5:4s

Core type: 5 - has a core need to be knowledgeable, in order to be safe.

Influenced by: 4 - has an additional drive to be special or different, in order to be noticed.

The need to be special softens 5s, taking them more into exploration of emotional authenticity. The dark arts will appeal to this forensic's quest to know; the desire to be unique will take their innovative sensitivity into the surreal and macabre; they forge ahead, where others might recoil.

Safety for the 5:4s comes from having explored the exposure they fear - emotional vulnerability is researched and resourced. They have empathy for the pain inherent in life and will be more emotional in their responses to it. Forewarned is forearmed in their world - knowing the worst and preparing for it is the policy of this realist.

The 4 influence on the 5 makes them more reclusive - introspection is essential, knowledge, an extreme pursuit. Immersion is absolute, 5:4s can become lost in the palace of their mind - at this point, the rest of life can become irrelevant.

5:6s

Core type: 5 - has a core need to be knowledgeable, in order to be safe.

Influenced by: 6 - has an additional drive towards order and belonging, in order to be secure.

The need for order sharpens the forensic laser. Curiosity is focused on solving problems and creating efficient systems. They cut to the chase and become the expert in order to get the job done. The drive to bring order, makes them more practical and pragmatic. They enjoy being the consultant on call.

Safety for 5:6s comes from knowing 'everything there is to know' about the potential vulnerabilities of their team, which can appear highly competitive. Whilst they have a strong sense of community connection, they also resist neediness and can be coolly dismissive, showing harsh impatience when the apparent ignorance of others obstructs their expertise.

The 6 influence on the 5 engages their supreme intellect in meeting the practical needs of the many - safety is found in enhancing the survival of the group.

The Teammate

6:5s

Core type: 6 - has a core need for order and belonging, in order to be secure.

Influenced by: 5 - has an additional need to be knowledgeable, in order to be safe.

The drive for safety through knowledge adds a layer of information-seeking and scepticism to the 6:5's need for belonging. Etiquette, convention and duty are key for ever-doubtful 6:5s. They need to know what is expected; and to check that others follow the rules.

Security for 6:5s comes from using a trustworthy, objective knowledge base to bring order out of chaos. Security comes from protocols and procedures which ensure conformity. Wisdom of the elders, respect for collective knowledge, organisational hierarchy give 6:5s structures on which they can depend.

The 5 influence on the 6 makes this teammate more private, reserved and self-effacing, with an abhorrence for showy attention seeking. Risk assessment is inbuilt for 6:5s who research the pitfalls thoroughly before making any choice.

6:7s

Core type: 6 - has a core need for order and belonging, in order to be secure.

Influenced by: 7 - has an additional need to be stimulated, in order to be safe.

The drive for stimulation draws the 6:7 towards others and there is generally a need to keep busy. Excitement will beckon; still checking for danger, they are more likely to 'push the envelope'.

Security comes from being part of the pack; taking repeated soundings for reassurance. Their code is one of loyalty and altruism - the needs of the many outweigh the needs of the few. They can be unexpectedly vocal, saying the things others wouldn't dream of putting into words.

The fun-seeking 7 brings out a silly side in 6:7s; they can clown about with glee - but only when they feel safe. Wacky humour and camaraderie typify 6:7s; making their 'group' laugh brings both security and entertainment.

The Adventurer

7:6s

Core type: 7 - has a core need to be stimulated, in order to be safe.

Influenced by: 6 - has an additional need for order and belonging, in order to be secure.

The need to belong attracts 7:6s to the fun they can have with others, where they can be found generating group hilarity or creating a zany itinerary.

Safety for 7:6s comes from the buzz of others' responses - and from the bulging calendar with never a dull day in sight. They are more likely to be the entertainer, they can become scattered - a veritable whirlwind of frantic activity. An escape plan from the mundanities of life keeps them safe from the abyss of an unstimulated mind.

The 6-based importance of trust brings loyalty to the fore for 7:6s who are more emotionally expressive, more sensitive to others and more risk averse in search of novel experience, seeking enjoyment rather than extreme thrills.

7:8s

Core type: 7 - has a core need to be stimulated, in order to be safe.

Influenced by: 8 - has an additional need for strength and power, in order to be in control.

The desire for power brings out the realist in entrepreneurial 7:8s, who seek stimulation through (often outrageous) projects which give them that feeling of being on top of the world.

Safety for 7:8s comes from stretching the limits of their strength: physically, mentally and emotionally, to experience everything the world has to offer and satisfy their need for excitement. These are likely to be the thrill-seekers: safety comes from demonstrating their own indomitability.

The 8-like need to take charge, makes 7:8s rather less sensitive, less likely to show vulnerability; they have a tough directness, verging on bluntness at times. They have a strong presence; they thrive on challenge.

The Champion

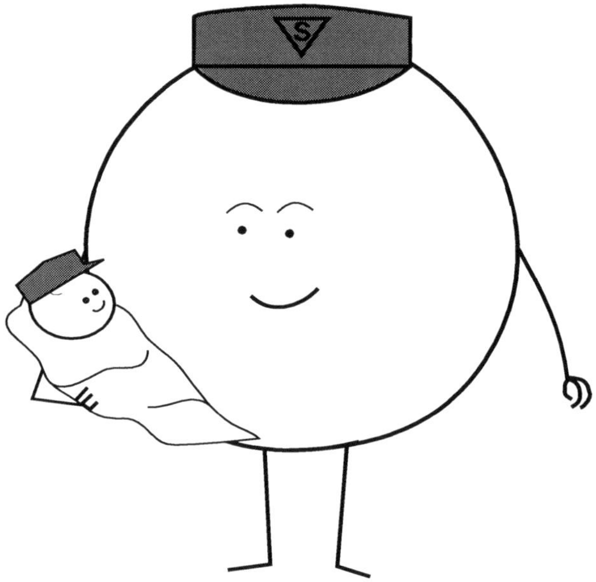

8:7s

Core type: 8 - has a core need for strength and power, in order to be in control.

Influenced by: 7 - has an additional need to be stimulated, in order to be safe.

The need for variety brings an energy to the 8. 8:7s become powerful, dynamic activators. They move mountains, driving projects forward with charismatic energy.

Control for 8:7s comes from their sense of being in command of everything in their world. The fear base of the 7 gives their power an edginess: clearly ready to confront a challenge, head-on; valiant in a crisis, they will do whatever it takes to protect their patch.

The 7-like need to be stimulated makes this 8 more overtly dominant, they are more likely to show anger: the champion of the battlefield - real or metaphorical.

8:9s

Core type: 8 - has a core need for strength and power, in order to be in control.

Influenced by: 9 - has an additional need to avoid conflict, in order to be in control.

The 9 influence on the 8 tempers the challenge of the champion. Strong and warm, with palpable power, they command by presence alone. They are more likely to settle for comfort over combat until threatened. Then, the power of the 8 mobilises; they will stop at nothing to look after their own.

Control for 8:9s comes from the passion they have for their people - family, friends or colleagues. They engulf their people with power; strength emanates from connection with those in their domain.

The 9 influence creates more internal control - they are less likely to show anger, more likely to compel. Their steady strength needs no announcing: they assume dominance with ease.

The Peacemaker

9:8s

Core type: 9 - has a core need to avoid conflict, in order to be in control.

Influenced by: 8 - has an additional need for strength and power, in order to be in control.

The 8 wing brings a power to the 9:8, which translates into a readiness to stand their ground and say what needs to be said. 9:8s are more dynamic, they have a steady determination, which fuels action - they are more likely to get things done and manage conflict should the need arise.

Control for 9:8s comes from a passionate core; being more comfortable with anger makes them confident, particularly if wellbeing, of self or others, is under threat. They harness it, registering views calmly, with gentle strength. They bring balance by facing challenge with the power of persuasion.

The 8 influence brings sociability and reduces inhibition, it draws the 9:8 into the world of action and consequence. Practical and pragmatic, they drive projects forward and make things happen. They make natural negotiators, handling conflict with poise.

9:1s

Core type: 9 - has a core need to avoid conflict, in order to be in control.

Influenced by: 1 - has an additional need to do the right thing and do it right, in order to be in control.

The 1 wing brings idealism to the harmony seeking 9. The desire to be 'good' makes 9:1s even more uncomfortable with conflict. At pains to avoid argument, they will disengage from the messiness of reality in order to nurture their dreams.

Control for 9:1s comes from managing themselves and avoiding discomfort. Gentle and affable, they see all shades of grey and listen with intent to understand. They weave ideas with an eye for pattern and purpose.

The 1 influence makes the 9:1 less likely to show anger; lower in energy and more passive, they can be easily distracted into pursuit of the non-essential. High standards make them self-critical. They sacrifice self, to keep the peace.

The Reformer

1:9s

Core type: 1 - has a core need to do the right thing and do it right, in order to be in control.

Influenced by: 9 - has an additional need to avoid conflict, in order to be in control.

The 9 wing softens the zealous 1, making 1:9s approachable and friendly. The desire for harmony brings restraint. 1:9s will attempt to suppress the fizz of frustration of life failing to meet their standards.

Control for 1:9s comes from maintaining their composure. They work hard to be seen to be fair and good. Their 9-wing desire to avoid conflict can translate into a stiffness, sometimes heard in clipped tones. Kind and humble, with a gentle touch - 1:9s want to do the right thing.

The 9 influence draws the 1 into big picture thinking; they are more likely to philosophise about a better world, than to get involved in the minutiae of creating it. Polite and dignified, 1:9s want to drive reform without losing connection.

1:2s

Core type: 1 - has a core need to do the right thing and do it right, in order to be in control.

Influenced by: 2 - has an additional need to be needed, in order to be loved.

The 2 wing brings emotion and action to the 1. 1:2s will seek approval as they strive to meet others' needs, but will be more ready to show frustration. They are compassionate and warm, driving improvement to serve the vulnerable or unloved.

Control for 1:2s comes from commitment to the cause and from galvanising of others by rolling up their sleeves alongside them. Leading by example, they will suffer much to be a worthy role model; they feel criticism and judgment keenly in their efforts to make the world a better place.

The 2 wing brings a pragmatism to the 1. 1:2s will settle for what is realistically achievable, whilst giving their all to make a difference. They are practical in outlook, less serious, more able to laugh at themselves along the way.

The Primal Drives

The Primal Drives
- Find your instinctual comfort zone

In addition to all the shades and nuances of types, wings, directions of movement, reactions to stress and need, there is an additional, fundamental influence on each type. This is separate to the types and can be seen and understood without knowing specific type, because the impact of this influence is generic.

This last layer of variation stems from our primal drives: to preserve self, apart from others; to create intimacy; and to socialise, as part of the group. All three drives arise in all of us, they are fundamental to existence.

We describe the three resulting variants as the solitary, intimate and social variants.
The premise here is that we all operate from all three drives, but that one becomes dominant, potentially as a result of early experiences. We can find that another of the drives may be underdeveloped, which can lead to imbalance.

The drives will have a priority order for each of us and the order remains the same throughout life. The impact of our primal drives can change, depending on our level of health and balance. At times we can be at our healthy best, making the most of all three drives to create a happy balance. At others, we can be out of balance and the our primal drive will be the one which shows up our personality stresses most vividly.

To identify our dominant variance, we ask ourselves which matters most, as we reflect on the following descriptions. We also notice imbalance - is there one drive which is significantly underdeveloped for us, in which case, are we neglecting it, to our cost?

The Solitary Variant

Solitary variants are most of all concerned with preserving self, rather than connecting with others. This does not mean that they are not sociable, that they don't like people, nor does it mean that they are introvert. It means that their prime drive is to ensure that they have everything they need for survival. Their attention, on entering a room, for example, will be on the temperature, lighting, comfort, accessibility of amenities. They want to know if their physical needs will be well catered for, irrespective of the presence or absence of other people.

When out of balance, this variant is most likely to become isolated, dismissing others as irrelevant or even harmful to their wellbeing. When unhealthy, solitary variants will create distress in their environment, as they become conflicted about the very thing that matters most. They may deprive themselves or over indulge their base needs, in a turbulent sense of never having enough to satisfy the need. They will have a strong sense of wanting to preserve their space and control their environment; but will be so fearful of losing this, that they bring about the very downfall they fear the most, by losing connection with other people, without whom they cannot actually survive.

Self-preservation will be the focus. This variant will lack the desire to have other people in their space, depending, to some degree, on the level of disruption they cause to the basic need supply. At its best, this will create a focus on the details which create healthy, pleasing environments, where physical needs are prioritised and met. It will also support a variant who is self-sufficient and is happy with their own space, not needing others to feel complete. Each type will bring its own spin to this, depending on the personality playing out.

The Intimate Variant

For the intimate variant, it is the close connection with others that matters most. This does not mean that they are averse to larger scale socialising, or that they cannot enjoy solitude and comfortable environments, but the prime drive for them is the depth and significance of their intimate relationships. On entering a room, they will be looking for the richest, most life-giving energy, the person with most interest, most potential to connect, in the room. This is regardless of people's position or ability to supply needs, it is solely about the potential to form meaningful, intimate bonds.

When unhealthy, the intimate variant may become overly intense, desperate for closeness, creating dependence or seeking out the emotionally vulnerable, 'feeding' on the feelings and neediness of others. This may be coupled with an equally strong pull to be free, an inability to cope with the long term emotional drain of such situations. They can suddenly abandon ship, becoming cold and unapproachable, or just disappearing when they are needed the most. They oscillate between finding new sources of emotional intimacy, and periods of reclusive isolation or over-socialising, to escape the closeness they lack the stamina to maintain.

Generally appreciative and approachable, this variant will tend to have an intensity about them; each person encountered is explored to gauge degree of 'match'. The gift of the intimate variant is to create deep, lasting relationships, to extend the height and plumb the depths of human experience, to hold others close at the moments that matter most. Intimate variants thrive on the sharing of confidences, on being there for others, day to day and at the time of greatest need. Deep down, this is stemming from a primal need for 'oneness'; a belief that the sense of complete unity with significant others is essential to life.

The Social Variant

The social variant is driven by the desire to be part of a group - to be an accepted, approved pack member. This does not mean that this variant is necessarily extrovert, or that they are not happy to spend time alone, but their primal instinct is to ensure that their group is strong and secure, and that they are well established within it. When they enter a room, they are more likely to pick up on where the power balance is, sensing influence and 'clout'; they will be drawn to the people best placed to meet their needs. Social variants acquire information naturally, networking and connecting through contacts and reputation.
It is important that they are seen and acknowledged by those who support their survival.

The social variant can become overly focused on the need to be included, to be part of a 'pack'. This can result in overdone, calculating networking, which becomes manipulative and results, ultimately, in rejection. The unhealthy social variant can lose their authenticity; driven to be accepted by others, they may contort themselves to do what they imagine the group requires for continued membership. Meaningful connection can be sacrificed; spreading themselves thinly, they do not want to miss an opportunity for group bonding. This becomes isolating; lacking closeness, or attempting to force allegiances, natural social bonds become contrived and they find themselves either rejecting their group or being barred from it.

At its best, the social instinct in this variant creates warmth and inclusion. They sense the power in the collective - the value of the individual coming to the fore in the context of a group where the whole is so much more than the sum of its parts. They bring the best out of diversity, sensing complementary gifts and spotting potential for mutual benefit. When healthy, the social variant will be very mindful of the vulnerable; they will direct the resources of the group to support and strengthen those in need. They will naturally expand possibilities and plan expansion, they optimise the capacity of the many to bring benefits for all.

How does this help?

So, how does this information help us to bring the best out of our type?

The first thing to consider is to check the balance of the three drives in your own experience; the following questions may help:

How happy are you to spend time alone? How do you feel about solitude?

How much do you seek out and enjoy intimate connection with others? How do you feel about meaningful relationships?

How often would you choose to be part of a group? How do you feel about social events and opportunities?

Notice what the responses to these questions tell you about the strength of each of these drives for you. Take a moment to reflect on the balance between the three - when you are at your best, and when you are out of sorts.

Knowing our primal drives enables us to make conscious choices about the situations and contexts which enable us to thrive. It can be equally powerful to understand the drives of others: we can let go of our need for significant people in our lives to be like ourselves. This information alone can release huge amounts of stress from strained professional and personal relationships, setting people free to be at their best.

Letting others know our preferences and need can have a significant impact on our wellbeing. For some, who have strong solitary and/or intimate drives, with low social drive, it is immensely stressful, for example, to feel under pressure to attend social events. Knowing the primal drives can make it easier to simply say "No", or to ensure that the situation includes some 'break out' time to recharge.

For others, with high social drives, loneliness can be a strong and poignant theme - solitude can feel threatening and harsh. For these, consciously choosing environments with a strong social base is helpful and reduces stress. Building in limited periods of solitude can then be considered, to develop greater balance.

The combinations and impact of these three drives are unique to each person, but will be playing out strongly in our lives, whether or not we have awareness of them. This insight makes sense of why situations have felt intensely uncomfortable to one person, whilst they are another's delight. Bringing this understanding into relationships, families and social or professional groups is hugely freeing - we stop imposing our world on others; everyone benefits as a result.

Dos and Don'ts

Dos and Don'ts
- Practical tips for optimising relationships
- Personal Plans to enhance each type's strengths

When we look at why our reactions to people elicit unexpectedly challenging responses, we find that the underlying principle is very simple. This principle involves the three directions of movement - which may be mental, emotional or physical. When we move mentally, we engage our mind and our thinking. Moving emotionally engages the heart and feelings. Moving physically, we see action: stemming from the gut, we move the body, engaging physically with life.

Each centre has a **primary direction** of movement. Heart types will 'move towards' others, emotionally, in the first instance, seeking love, attention, acknowledgement. This may also involve mental or physical movement into others' space. When out of balance this can become suffocating, cloying, even aggressive in the need to outdo others.

Head types will tend to 'move away', mentally at least: seeking safety, they retreat internally to keep their inner world secure. We may see this 'away' movement as physical or emotional remoteness. When out of balance, this distance becomes cold, aloof; head types can appear disinterested or dismissive.

Gut types will 'move against' as a first instinct, physically battling the elements to gain control of their inner or outer world. The gut drives action, which may also involve mental or emotional duelling, at least in the form of heavy persuasion, to effect change. When out of balance, this can become aggressive, passive-aggressive, bullying and stubborn.

The primary direction of movement will play an important part in creating the 'dance', which then unfolds between the types. We start to understand more easily why some dances will be smoother, others will be more zesty or feisty, depending on our own patterns and on the awareness we have of how others move.

If, for example, our personality type needs to move away when under stress; if we are out of balance and we are interacting with someone who needs to move towards, we will struggle unless we know what is playing out and have some guidance as to how best to respond.

Taking an example: if a 2 is interacting with a 5, we may find a challenge to be overcome. The 2 moves towards others as a heart type to pursue the one they wish to serve. The 5, as a head type, moves away from others. So we may see the 2 chasing, in order to help and the 5 metaphorically (or literally!) running away.

Heart types

When heart types are out of balance, they 'move towards' others, primarily; their behaviour becomes needy, desiring of attention and acknowledgement. We need to be aware that this will trigger responses in ourselves, especially if our pattern is different. Their overt neediness will also prevent them from giving love or attention to others; as with all types, when unhealthy, they take away from others what they most want for themselves.

For types who are more self contained, it may be a real stretch to 'move towards' someone at this point - everything in our system may ‘move us away' or even 'against' in reaction to their need. 'Moving towards' is exactly what is needed to ease and enhance the relationship.

2s - The Helpers

Dos...

1. Appreciate them, let them know they are needed and loved, especially when you least feel like it! *"Appreciate me. Recognise what I do for you. Thank me. It really is that simple."*

2. Encourage them to say 'No'. Practise it with them, be playful about it and reassure them when they do - remind them that they have to look after themselves in order to give to others.

3. Seek their help when you can, they will be truly delighted that they can be of use to you and will leave no stone unturned on your behalf. *"I want to be the one who helps people to find things and get something done - like when my children ask for help with homework."*

4. Gently, if possible, approach the concept of healthy selfishness - that every act is selfish in nature. If they help, they do so because of the pleasure they get from being needed.

5. Help them to enjoy life and live life for themselves, not just for what they can do for others. *"I love sharing a common bond. I love knowing that I have such wonderful family and friends. It's something I need to remind myself of sometimes, when I am feeling low."*

6. Encourage them to have fun for fun's sake and to allow themselves to 'be' rather than 'do'. Show them how this nourishes them and allows them to have more to give others. *"I love having fun and lots of it, whether it be singing, dancing, entertaining, I love generally having a good time - socialising and having fun."*

7. Reassure them that if you do something without their help, this does not mean you don't love or appreciate them.

8. Help them to acknowledge their own needs, although they may resist the word 'need' and may feel this takes away from their sense of self. *"At the time, I may not realise and appreciate it, but I love it when - I am in a mood, we have had a disagreement - and my husband forces me to smile, gives me a hug and makes me feel so good again."*

9. Guide them to understand that sharing their needs and challenges with others makes them stronger and builds relationships, by allowing others to be the 'givers', instead of always being the 'receivers'. *"When I'm not at my best, I need people to reassure me and help me to understand my own needs."*
"I like people to understand that I am not always on top form or always smiling and positive. It's times like that, that I don't want to be the one who does everything. But that's when it gets tricky because I change my rules!"

10. Enable them to ask for what they want: show them how assertive requests build respect and enrich relationships.

Don'ts...

Don't forget to show your thanks: in word, gesture or deed. 2s will do anything for you but they live for the appreciation this brings.

"What upsets me is when I am taken for granted: when I am not appreciated and my efforts go unrecognised."

Don't make them feel redundant - this is agony to a 2. Everything they need to believe about themselves comes from their absolute 'knowing' that others are needy and that they are the suppliers to meet those needs.

Don't criticise them; instead show them how to help or serve even more effectively.

"It upsets me when people have misinterpreted my desire to help and organise as interfering and they don't understand my motives."

REFLECTION

What does this section on 2s teach you about yourself?

What might you do differently to enhance your relationships with potential 2s?

Personal plan for 2s

If you are a 2, the very best thing you can do, to supercharge your ability to help others, is to help yourself first. Then, and only then, can you flourish in your ability to assist others. Otherwise, you may find yourself doing things unwillingly or with frustration and you can't be at your best. To be at your best, you need to be loving every minute of helping others and then everything you do will be done with good grace. You need to be at the top of your own daily 'to do' list.

Are you currently even on your 'to do' list?
What do you do, just for yourself, every single day?
How would helping yourself first enhance your ability to help others?

The very best help we can give another is to empower them to help themselves. Tempting as it is, giving a starving person a fish feeds them only for one day and you only get to help that one person by feeding them daily. Teaching a person to fish will feed them for a lifetime and you can then help so many others to do the same.

Are you currently doing for others, something they could potentially do for themselves?
What could you hand over or teach to others?
How would empowering others increase their appreciation of you?

What actions will you take to make the most of your gifts and strengths as a 2?

In one week's time, having made these changes:
What will others see?
What will others hear?
How will it feel?

In a month's time:
How will it look?
Sound?
Feel?

After six months:
What will people see?
Hear?
How will you be feeling in six months' time?

And after a year of making these changes:
What will it look like?
What will it sound like?
What will you be feeling?

3s - The Achievers

Dos...

1. Acknowledge their successes, especially if they are boasting, it reassures them; they thrive on respect.

"What I like people to do is to reassure me by noticing my abilities".

2. Be playful in bringing them back into balance: gentle, warm reminders that they are not quite the "be all and end all", all of the time, in everything, helps them to respond in kind.

3. Encourage them to acknowledge themselves for who they are as opposed to what they may have achieved.

4. Tell them what you admire and appreciate about them, especially when they least expect it; it builds their sense of worth - which is more fragile than appearances might suggest.

5. Nurture their ability to relax and 'be', rather than needing to always 'do'; they benefit from realising that this recharges their batteries, making them more efficient and effective.

6. Help them to connect with what really matters to them: help them to recognise the aspects of life that they may otherwise neglect.

"What enhances my relationship with others is a warm-hearted, ready to laugh outlook."

7. Help them to realise their interdependence: their success relies on others, they are one of a team.

8. Encourage them to recognise and acknowledge others' gifts and success, building reciprocity. Help them to realise that appreciation of others' achievements enhances their own brilliance.

9. Show them that sharing experiences of failure makes them greater. Reflect back to them that the honesty of these moments grows respect through relationship.

10. Give them balanced, constructive feedback, with focus on what they have done well and offering areas for development with an overt intent to help them to become even more successful.

Don'ts...

Don't burst their boasting balloon. Humiliation, especially in public, will stifle their sense of success, resulting in even greater competitive attack.

Don't try to outdo a 3 - it will only stimulate more imbalance. Encourage a supportive relationship, in which competition and success is of mutual benefit.

Don't criticise, instead, acknowledge their goals and give supportive suggestions to help them improve.

"Emotional coldness or aloofness hurts me".

REFLECTION

What does this section on 3s teach you about yourself?

What might you do differently to enhance your relationships with potential 3s?

Personal plan for 3s

If you are a 3, appreciating that "the whole is greater than the sum of the parts" maximises your success. Enhancing all areas of your life; acknowledging the gifts that others bring and embracing failure are all essential to creating the route to ultimate achievement. Ego-driven success will be narrow and leads to neglect and regret. You need to consciously develop balance, relaxing enough to allow others' success to augment your own - the riches of life will then be fully yours.

What areas of life do you tend to neglect?
What might you regret if you carry on just the way you are?
What relationships might you give more attention?

Focusing on image and prestige whilst disguising failure creates a veneer, which lacks heart and misses the meaning of true success. "All that glitters is not gold" warns us: scratch the surface and a different truth emerges. Pure gold lies within; the 3's quest is to mine the depths of their own capacity to love.

How much do you love and acknowledge the people in your life?
How much do you appreciate others' contribution to your success?
How open are you with your failures?

What actions will you take to make the most of your gifts and strengths as a 3?

In one week's time, having made these changes:
What will others see?
What will others hear?
How will it feel?

In a month's time:
How will it look?
Sound?
Feel?

After six months:
What will people see?
Hear?
How will you be feeling in six months' time?

And after a year of making these changes:
What will it look like?
What will it sound like?
What will you be feeling?

4s - The Individualists

Dos...

1. Allow them to feel the full range of their emotions and appreciate their emotional integrity.

"I like people to be transparent ... those that are genuine, open and honest."

2. Give them time to find their own way back into balance.

"When I'm under pressure I like to withdraw."

3. Value their contributions and insights; seek out their unique take on life.

"My best relationships are with those who have a world view. I am attracted to people who are deep and seek meaning in things."

4. Let them know that you understand how they get to the heart of situations even if what they bring is not comfortable.

5. Embrace their gift to spot the flaw in your ideas; ask them to troubleshoot in ways that work for you.

6. Encourage them to harness their creativity to solve problems they spot; honour the beauty of their inspired self.

7. Gently reassure them; show compassion for their plight. Accept their perspective no matter how different it is from your own.

8. Accept that they will feel lonely and yet they will often choose to be alone.

9. Lighten them up with humour, where possible; invite a sense of fun.

10. Help them to know that valuing everyone heals the wounded heart.

Don'ts...

Don't try to downplay their drama, it will fuel their envy.

Don't attempt to pull them out of their pain, be there to support when they are ready.

Don't reject their message; there is a truth at its core.

"I am most hurt by people who reject me."

REFLECTION

What does this section on 4s teach you about yourself?

What might you do differently to enhance your relationships with potential 4s?

Personal plan for 4s

If you are a 4, appreciating and valuing your worth enables you to fully embrace your uniqueness, without the need for validation from others. Accepting help from others rather than withdrawing from life will reduce that feeling of isolation and loneliness. Courage to embrace the full range of emotions takes energy and resilience – remember resilient people are confident enough to call on their support network – they do not feel they have to do it all alone. Calling on your support helps to lessen the 'lonely' feelings; it helps you to feel loved and valued and to become solution focused.

How much do you currently value yourself?
What do you do every day to value yourself and to value the special qualities of others?
How would helping yourself first, attract people to you?

Focusing on what you want helps to visualise the beauty of how life can be rather than the misery and fragility that negative thoughts can create. Embracing life without support can be frightening and lonely. Facing your fears and moving forward is enabling and brave; it allows you to be a power for change and innovation.

How much do you love and appreciate the people in your life?
How much do you take time to appreciate the good in your life and the world around you?
How might appreciating what's good in life attract more love into your life?

What actions will you take to make the most of your gifts and strengths as a 4?

In one week's time, having made these changes:
What will others see?
What will others hear?
How will it feel?

In a month's time:
How will it look?
Sound?
Feel?

After six months:
What will people see?
Hear?
How will you be feeling in six months' time?

And after a year of making these changes:
What will it look like?
What will it sound like?
What will you be feeling?

Head types

When head types are out of balance, they 'move away' from others, their behaviour will become aloof, distancing themselves; we need to be aware that this may trigger responses in us. Their protective, edgy dissociation will unsettle the sense of safety for others; when unhealthy, they take away from others what they most want for themselves.

For types who are less self-contained, it may be uncomfortable to allow the distance at this point - everything in our system may 'move us towards' or even 'against' in reaction to their disconnection. Space to 'move away' is exactly what is needed to allow a sense of safety to return.

5s - The Forensics

Dos...

1. Understand their need for space, physically and emotionally, distance allows them to think clearly and to be objective.

"I like being part of a group when working together... (as long as it is) purposeful, open and without rules... I'm happy to lead because then I'm at the front, not the centre."

2. Welcome their thorough exposition and exploration of a subject; they do know a LOT and they will not be satisfied with a superficial understanding.

"Don't accuse me of being fussy, I am not fussy at all, it's just that I won't accept second best if I know how to do/get the best thing."

3. Respect their 'absolutes', if you want to challenge a judgment, bring information to support that challenge.

4. Value their expertise; make the most of their knowledge and desire to learn more.

5. Speak objectively, be brief and economical.

"Hard to think of any 'Dos'. Maybe, 'Do give me the benefit of the doubt'."

6. Understand that when they break rapport with you, they are subconsciously trying to keep themselves safe.

7. Appreciate their need to know, if they sound competitive or judgemental, they are just trying reassure themselves that their superior knowledge base is secure.

8. Support them, in simple practical ways, with no strings attached.

9. Manage your own emotions, keep your language fact based and calm.

"My ideal social group would have two, maybe three people. Don't make me the centre of attention, it's as bad as physical pain."

9. Encourage them to go with their 'gut' instinct, taking them beyond logic.

10. Stay self-sufficient and calm on the rare occasions when they show their emotions.

Don'ts...

Don't interpret their blunt objectivity as a personal criticism - it is just their uncensored analysis of the situation.

Don't overwhelm them with emotion and neediness, it scares them.

Don't surprise them outside their fortress of knowledge - the exposure is excruciating.

"Don't invite me to parties ... They feel unnatural, full of pretence and I have no idea what to say or do."

REFLECTION

What does this section on 5s teach you about yourself?

What might you do differently to enhance your relationships with potential 5s?

Personal plan for 5s

If you are a 5, to maximise your intellect, it is important to address your physical and mental wellbeing, finding ways to rest the mind and body, enabling it to be even more bountiful – "The field that is rested produces a bountiful crop"'. Whilst being alone enables you to assimilate information, collaboration could bring broader thinking and even better results, but patience is important. Not everyone will process so quickly, but "Good things come to those who wait."

What areas of your wellbeing do you tend to neglect?
How might this impact on your capacity to learn and move forward?
What relationships might you start to trust?

Acknowledge the 'mastery mindset' that we are never done, there is always more to learn. This approach need not be frightening but exciting. There will always be more exploration: the universe is constantly expanding.

How much do you show emotional acknowledgement to the people in your life?
How much do you seek others' contribution and always keep the end in mind?
How open are you with your shortcomings, how comfortable are you that you don't know it all?

What actions will you take to make the most of your gifts and strengths as a 5?

In one week's time, having made these changes:
What will others see?
What will others hear?
How will it feel?

In a month's time:
How will it look?
Sound?
Feel?

After six months:
What will people see?
Hear?
How will you be feeling in six months' time?

And after a year of making these changes:
What will it look like?
What will it sound like?
What will you be feeling?

6s - The Teammates

Dos...

1. Say what you mean and mean what you say; they are very attuned to body language and need communication to be clear and trustworthy.

"I like people to be reliable and straight with me, I like them to be clear and concise and to help me to see the bigger picture."

2. Listen to their fears and worries and allow them to vent; their concerns will have validity.

"When I am feeling out of sorts, I like people to listen to my fears and frustrations; I like to get things off my chest."

3. Demonstrate reliability, they need to know they can depend on you.

4. Acknowledge their contribution, quietly, simply and with sincerity.

5. Appreciate their earthy, somewhat bizarre sense of humour: they will laugh at the strangest of things.

6. Stand by them; loyalty is everything to them.

"I like being with like-minded people...something in common... watching our football team together... playing in a band... I feel really good being part of the same team."

7. Help them to trust their intuition; they have a 'sixth sense' - encourage them to follow it, no matter how illogical it may appear.

8. Challenge them to reach for their potential.

9. Tease them out of their comfort zone, bring new experiences and adventures their way.

10. Steady them: show them how to find their calm.

Don'ts...

Don't downplay their fears, which may appear dramatic and overreactive.

"It might seem like I'm complaining but in my eyes, I'm just saying..."

Don't let them down.

"I hate it when people don't follow through on their promises. I feel let down and annoyed."

Don't single them out in the group for special attention.

REFLECTION

What does this section on 6s teach you about yourself?

What might you do differently to enhance your relationships with potential 6s?

Personal plan for 6s

If you are a 6, expanding your comfort zone and learning to take calculated risks will enhance your confidence and build your success. Whilst the talent of the team is important, don't let your desire to blend in and keep your world safe, limit your life experiences. Sometimes, standing out, being noticed for who you are, is a very healthy thing.

In what areas of your life do you limit yourself?
Where do you need to trust yourself more?
What relationships might you trust more?

Whilst organisation and structure provide efficiency, it can, when out of balance, become rigid and limiting, with no room for spontaneity. Always questioning others' motives creates apprehension and distance. Learning to trust others and to rely on your own gut instinct are essential to your decision-making ability.

How much do you trust the people in your life?
How much do you acknowledge your own contribution to the success of the team?
How open are you to expanding your comfort zone and embracing new experiences?

What actions will you take to make the most of your gifts and strengths as a 6?

In one week's time, having made these changes:
What will others see?
What will others hear?
How will it feel?

In a month's time:
How will it look?
Sound?
Feel?

After six months:
What will people see?
Hear?
How will you be feeling in six months' time?

And after a year of making these changes:
What will it look like?
What will it sound like?
What will you be feeling?

7s - The Adventurers

Dos...

1. Encourage them to relax and find inner calm; help them to see that this will heighten their enjoyment of life.

"Surrounding myself with calm people who are unlike me, enhances my wellbeing."

2. Enjoy their stories, engage their sense of fun.

"I love it when people listen to my stories and life plans and encourage my dreams and ambitions, even if they seem a bit ridiculous and you know that they will all change next week. Encourage my fairy tales!"

3. Help them to focus on one thing at a time; make that thing as real and colourful as possible.

4. Encourage them to find satisfaction in finishing things, seeing them through to the end.

"I get frustrated with myself for not getting enough done."

5. Make the most of their imagination and sparkle, channel their 'outside the box' thinking to generate ideas and innovate.

6. Give them variety and challenge; keep things fresh and 'spicy'.

7. Ground them in reality, help them to develop stamina for the duller parts of life - but do it gently, with humour if possible.

8. Coax them towards structure, show them how it gives them greater scope for fun.

9. Help them to share their troubles; they will feel a pressure to entertain and may struggle to let you know that they too feel low sometimes.

10. Focus them on the now: show them how much more exciting life is when one is fully present, even with the simplest and plainest of experiences.

Don'ts...

Don't bore them; their minds move at lightning speed.

Don't spoil their fun - pace it and balance it, if necessary, but don't throw cold water on the party!

Don't overwhelm them with intense emotion or negativity.

"When I am under pressure or not at my best... Give me space."
"... negativity weighs me down... I like to feel alive, not with a big rain cloud over my head."

REFLECTION

What does this section on 7s teach you about yourself?

What might you do differently to enhance your relationships with potential 7s?

Personal plan for 7s

If you are a 7, the excitement of life and thoughts of 'what might be' can be curtailed by frenetic activity and a manic mentality. Learning to plan and become more organised, may appear boring but might well enhance your success and enable you to accomplish more of those fantastic life plans.

What areas of your life do you neglect?
What might you regret if you carry on just the way you are?
What relationships need more attention?

Remember we are human 'beings' not human 'doings'. 7s in particular, can spend time 'doing' rather than 'being' in their quest for excitement. Happiness is not something we 'do', it is something we have to 'be'. If you are not careful you may run yourself ragged in your quest to do everything and not miss out on anything. Learning stillness and mindfulness enables you to be present and enjoy the moment, rather than always moving on to 'the next thing'.

How much time do you spend with the important people in your life?
How much do you listen to others and consider their needs, even if it is painful?
How much do you address your development needs ?

What actions will you take to make the most of your gifts and strengths as a 7?

In one week's time, having made these changes:
What will others see?
What will others hear?
How will it feel?

In a month's time:
How will it look?
Sound?
Feel?

After six months:
What will people see?
Hear?
How will you be feeling in six months' time?

And after a year of making these changes:
What will it look like?
What will it sound like?
What will you be feeling?

Gut types

When gut types are out of balance, they 'move against' others, their behaviour will become resistant or strained, desiring control; this will trigger responses in us. Their desire to take charge, subtly or overtly, will prevent them from giving control to others; when unhealthy, they too, take away from others what they most want for themselves.

For types who are more self-contained, or seeking to move towards, it may be a challenge to 'move against' someone at this point - everything in our system may 'move us away' or 'towards' in reaction to their need. 'Moving against' is needed, to challenge the imbalance and restore harmony.

8s - The Champions

Dos...

1. Be direct with them; they will respect your strength.

"I love people to be honest, open and direct, even when what they say/believe contradicts me."

2. Share your vulnerabilities with them, they take care of their people.

3. Show them that you're on their side: you're either with them, or against them.

4. Stand your ground: face them squarely and engage.

5. Encourage their tenderness: affirm their gentleness as a strength.

6. Respect their domain; control of their territory is paramount.

"I sometimes need a minute to myself, after which I like people who mean something to me to show affection or care, or ask how I am."

7. Admire their courage; enjoy their tales of victory and challenges overcome.

8. Engage their warrior spirit: they love a noble fight.

9. Accept them as they are: what you see is what you get.

"I don't hide my emotions well, nor do I really try to hide them. It's more endearing to show the good the bad and the ugly... Well that's what I tell myself!"

10. Be bold, be valiant; take life on with them, shoulder to shoulder.

Don'ts...

Don't vacillate; they will see this as betrayal.

"I can't stand people who sit on the fence or tell people what they want to hear rather than the truth. I don't like being around people who pretend that things are fine all the time, when they aren't."

Don't take their assertiveness personally; don't assume aggression when they are just making their views known.

Don't try to dominate: you won't win!

REFLECTION

What does this section on 8s teach you about yourself?

What might you do differently to enhance your relationships with potential 8s?

Personal plan for 8s

If you are an 8, listening to and appreciating the viewpoints of those around you might add to your own strength. Having an opposing viewpoint need not be a threat to you: a healthy challenge may build the strength of your whole group – remember, there can be power in a gentle approach.

What areas do you tend to neglect?
What might you regret if you carry on just the way you are?
What relationships might you view more favourably now?

Calm confidence shows strength. Channeling and controlling the mighty powerhouse within you will empower others rather than scaring them away. They will know you 'have their back' and will give their all to you in return.

How tender and gentle are you with the people in your life?
How much do you appreciate and acknowledge others' viewpoints?
How open are you with your shortcomings?

What actions will you take to make the most of your gifts and strengths as an 8?

In one week's time, having made these changes:
What will others see?
What will others hear?
How will it feel?

In a month's time:
How will it look?
Sound?
Feel?

After six months:
What will people see?
Hear?
How will you be feeling in six months' time?

And after a year of making these changes:
What will it look like?
What will it sound like?
What will you be feeling?

9s - The Peacemakers

Dos...

1. Encourage their playful side - fun is something they may neglect.

2. Be aware of their sensitivity - they generally don't show it, but loud voices, harsh tones, extremes of emotion are all felt very deeply.

"I love people who are positive and always see the best in others. I enjoy being around people who are relaxed and open natured."

3. Encourage them to embrace difficult situations, they have a gift for facilitation and negotiation.

4. Give them time alone to recharge: being with people is draining.

"I prefer to be left alone to calmly ... (get things done) so I don't feel too much pressure."

5. Give them full attention when they speak; they can be wordy but it means a great deal when someone really listens.

"When I am under pressure, emotionally overwhelmed, I like someone to hold a caring space for me, to listen to me..."

6. Help them to focus on what they want and to take steps, however small, towards that.

7. Coach rather than tell: they won't be told what to do, despite their easy going appearance.

8. Encourage them to articulate their physical responses to situations; they suppress emotional reactions for fear of 'rocking the boat'.

9. 'See' their contribution and reflect it back to them; they may feel like a 'non-entity'.

10. Encourage 9s to engage with the richness of life; they need support to invest fully in their physical, mental and emotional experience.

"For private matters, I prefer private, 1 to 1 conversations with close friends and family."

Don'ts…

Don't laugh at them when they are angry: it is cruelest form of torture - this is when they feel completely vulnerable.

Don't take them for granted; they hate to feel used.

"I feel hurt when I've been ignored, excluded, alienated or cut off in any way…"

Don't be aggressive around them; conflict is their deepest fear.

REFLECTION

What does this section on 9s teach you about yourself?

What might you do differently to enhance your relationships with potential 9s?

Personal plan for 9s

If you are a 9, mellow affability can create indecision and apparent indifference. Welcoming change and diversity is the source of true and lasting harmony.

What areas of you life do you tend to neglect?
What might you regret if you carry on just the way you are?
What relationships, with personalities different to your own, might you give more attention?

Neglecting self in a quest to 'keep the peace' does not serve 9s - watch for this pattern; it will make you less able to do things well, you will find resentment builds and energy drains away.

How much do you love and acknowledge yourself?
How much do you engage with others' needs?
How well do you develop yourself - how energised are you in this pursuit?

What actions will you take to make the most of your gifts and strengths as a 9?

In one week's time, having made these changes:
What will others see?
What will others hear?
How will it feel?

In a month's time:
How will it look?
Sound?
Feel?

After six months:
What will people see?
Hear?
How will you be feeling in six months' time?

And after a year of making these changes:
What will it look like?
What will it sound like?
What will you be feeling?

1s - The Reformers

Dos...

1. Reassure them; they are very hard on themselves.

2. Help them to relax and have fun; they will tend to be over-serious.

"Ensure that I am not being a workaholic and make sure I take time out for ... (others) and myself and let my hair down."

3. Help them to speak assertively - they may struggle to say what they think, for fear of judgement.

4. Appreciate their high standards and the sacrifices they make to achieve them.

5. Share the load with them; they can easily feel isolated and they will take responsibility for everything.

6. Be honest, be fair but be gentle: they are extremely sensitive to criticism.

"What do I want from people? Be honest, be organised, be on time!"

7. Help them to see others' perspectives and values; they need support to feel compassion for those who behave differently from themselves.

"If I am struggling to make a relationship work, then reminding me to put myself in their position can quite often make me see them in a new light."

8. If you have a challenge to bring, ask permission to be frank; then tell it to them straight.

9. Help them to see when 'good enough' is good enough.

10. Encourage them to embrace the power of positive focus - reassure them that focusing on the good will improve performance, not detract from it.

Don'ts...

Don't criticise them in public, they will hear feedback very humbly when it is delivered privately for their greater good.

Don't mask the truth; hidden motives are seen as a betrayal.

"I hate it when people are dishonest, because I have such a strong moral code. I can't stand insincerity as a personal trait."

Don't assume that the repressed anger you may sense is about you; it will invariably stem from their harsh judgement of themselves.

"When I am out of balance, what I really want people to do, is not notice! If I'm not at my best, I feel I am letting people down, and the last thing I would want anyone to do would be to know about it."

REFLECTION

What does this section on 1s teach you about yourself?

What might you do differently to enhance your relationships with potential 1s?

Personal plan for 1s

If you are a 1, you will be constantly judging yourself as 'good' or 'bad'; learning to relax and enjoy life is good for you and those around you: embrace the fun!

How could you be kinder to yourself?
How could you allow more fun and frivolity into your life?
How could you lighten up the relationships in your life?

An open, growth mindset approach to continual learning, moves a 1 from judgement to mastery – getting it wrong is not 'bad' ; it is essential to continuous improvement.

How much do you trust the people in your life?
How much do you allow imperfection in your life?
How open are you to receiving feedback?

What actions will you take to make the most of your gifts and strengths as a 1?

In one week's time, having made these changes:
What will others see?
What will others hear?
How will it feel?

In a month's time:
How will it look?
Sound?
Feel?

After six months:
What will people see?
Hear?
How will you be feeling in six months' time?

And after a year of making these changes:
What will it look like?
What will it sound like?
What will you be feeling?

Author Biographies

Amanda Maney is an Assistant to the Principal of the lead school for a Teaching School Alliance with over 20 years' experience working with primary school children.
She is an accredited Life Coach, an Advanced EFT practitioner, and Matrix Re-imprinting practitioner with training also in Solution Focused Brief Therapy, NLP and Journey Therapy.

Amanda has found Enneagram wisdom invaluable in her coaching-based approach to enabling and personalising children's learning and also in her wider work: training, coaching and facilitating teams and individuals.

'Know thyself' is central to her approach - self awareness creates the springboard for children and adults alike. Amanda's prime directive is personal empowerment: creating success by synergy and harnessing enthusiasm to expand potential. Amanda and her husband live in the North West of England which has been home to her since leaving her birthplace, London in 1986.

Rachel Watson is a successful lifestyle and business coach and trainer. She has 20-years' experience of working within the corporate arena and more than a decade as a professional coach.

Rachel is an accredited Executive Coach with the Association for Coaching, an accredited NLP and Stress Management practitioner, Resilience Trainer and Wellbeing Lecturer, accredited AAMET EFT Advanced practitioner, Matrix Re-imprinting practitioner, Reiki Master, and RMT provider, a member of Mensa and a member of The Institute for Learning.

Rachel is passionate about the importance of wellbeing. As a working mother of 4 grown up children, she knows firsthand the challenges of juggling life demands and a rewarding career, whilst raising a family. Rachel lives in the North West of England with her husband.

29476368R00072

Printed in Great Britain
by Amazon